Rowdy Rousey

Mike Straka

TRIUMPH
BOOKS

This book is dedicated to my daughters, Maxine and Olive; I hope that Ronda Rousey's story inspires you to not only believe in yourselves, but to dream big and love your life. And to Renzo Gracie, for always inspiring me to be better every day, and for allowing your academy to be my second home.

This book is available in quantity at special discounts for your group or organization. For further information, contact:

Triumph Books LLC
814 North Franklin Street
Chicago, Illinois 60610
(312) 337–0747
www.triumphbooks.com

Printed in U.S.A.

ISBN: 978-1-62937-239-6

Design by Patricia Frey
Cover design by Preston Pisellini

Photographs courtesy of AP Images (pages 3–4, 7, 11, 17, 20–21, 23, 25–26, 29, 31, 40, 42–43, 45, 51–54, 56–57, 59–60, 65–66, 68, 72, 74, 77, 79, 80, 83, 85–86, 93–98, 101, 103, 105, 114, 116, 118, 120, 122, 125–127), USA Today Sports Images (pages 9, 27–28, 35–36, 39, 47, 67, 70–71, 76, 89, 109, 113), Newscom (pages 12, 22, 30, 99, 102, 106, 119), and Icon Sportswire (page 18).

Ronda Rousey confronts Stephanie McMahon during a surprise, explosive appearance at Wrestlemania XXXI, on March 29, 2015 in Santa Clara, California.

Ronda Rousey gets focused prior to her
UFC 157 battle with Liz Carmouche.

Contents

Foreword

Ronda Rousey is an inspiring woman who set a goal to achieve in an industry that didn't exist.

She sacrificed everything to perfect a skill, just for the sake of being great. There was no fame, there was no money, there was not even a platform.

Let me remind you, the UFC, until just recently, vowed to never have women in MMA.

The martial arts, throughout the history of time, have largely been folklore. The heroes that you have heard about from Chuck Norris to Bruce Lee are wimps and frauds and charlatans, as it pertains to actually being able to physically dominate an opponent in hand to hand unarmed combat.

You will often hear about a guy who knows secret moves, trains in an undisclosed location, and has learned a skill that was passed down from his great grandfather. Everything you've ever heard about as it pertains to these types of mythical figures, are skills that are *actually* possessed by Ronda Rousey.

The most successful people in the world will tell you, "Don't do it for the money, follow your passion, and the money will take care of itself." That is truly what happened with Ronda. She had no master plan. She only had a goal and a vision of being the best at what she does.

Present time looks very favorably upon Ronda. She is an icon, a star, and a champion. But like a fine wine she will only get better with time. She paved the way for women everywhere on an international level.

People aspire to be like her. Men and women study her films to learn her techniques. But the story of Ronda Rousey should not be one about victories and armbars.

The story should be about a woman with a dream, who persevered at all costs, and changed not only a sport, but a gender forever. ■

—Chael Sonnen

Chael Sonnen flexes during the weigh-in for UFC Night 26 in August 2013.

Introduction

Interviewing the Baddest Woman on the Planet

In 2012 Ronda Rousey was preparing to fight Miesha Tate for the Strikeforce world women's bantamweight title on the Showtime premium cable network. I was co-host on Spike TV's *MMA Uncensored Live,* and was invited to Rousey's training camp to do an interview.

I had already had an interview with Tate in the can, in which Tate made appearances at various Las Vegas fight shops, signing autographs and smiling for pictures with dozens of fans everywhere she went. She was relishing the attention a fight with Rousey was providing, both from fans and media, and she was doing a great job handling it all.

When I arrived with my camera crew at Rousey's gym, to say the future Baddest Woman on the Planet was not happy to see me would be an understatement. While her fight manager and her BJJ trainer both told me everything was "good to go," somehow my interview subject was never informed.

To her, it looked like an ambush.

There she was, grappling with men, sweating and bleeding in between bouts of tears, and she was cleaning the mat with them. She was doing an ironman drill, where every minute or so a fresh grappler would jump in. This went on for 30 minutes as my camera crew and I milled about.

With every tap, Rousey would get up and glare at me.

It was unnerving, to say the least. Suddenly, one of the men accidentally kneed Ronda in the crotch. She screamed in pain and tears welled up in her eyes. "I'm sorry," he said. Ronda went red.

"Don't you ever say sorry to me again," she said through sobs. "Let's go."

Immediately as the two locked arms, Ronda executed one of the most beautiful *Harai Goshis* I've ever seen in my life. A *Harai Goshi* is a sweeping hip toss, where a judo player sweeps the leg while simultaneously throwing someone down over one's hip. It's quick and looks like the stuff of action movies. Ronda finished the throw with her now-patented armbar, and he tapped.

When she got up, she turned and glared at me. I thought, *I'm next.*

When practice was over Ronda disappeared into the locker room. One of the women from the gym followed her in and quickly went out, got into her car, and drove off.

Great, I thought. *We lost her.* I feared Rousey was sneaking out the back door and we wouldn't get the interview

Rousey holds her championship belt before a weigh-in at the MGM Grand Garden Arena in September 2015.

that I flew out to Los Angeles from New York to obtain. I panicked a little, because I told the executives at Spike TV I had the interview locked down.

There were three cameramen and an audio engineer with me, and those guys weren't cheap. In TV, guys get paid even if the show doesn't happen. In spite of my inner turmoil, I kept my cool and assured everyone that the interview would be fine.

"Keep setting up," I said calmly, as if this happened all the time. The guys went about setting up their lights and cameras.

By then I had interviewed nearly every single UFC champion for over a decade. I began covering mixed martial arts when I was the weekend sports guy at Fox News Channel at UFC 32 in June 2001. The winners that night are a who's who of UFC legends—some of which are Hall of Famers today. They were B.J. Penn, Tito Ortiz, Pat Miletich, Josh Barnett, Caol Uno, Vladimir

Matyushenko, and Ricco Rodriguez, who beat none other than Andrei Arlovski that night.

From there I hosted *Fox Fight Game*, *Fighting Words* on HDNet, *TapouT Radio* on SiriusXM, *MMA Uncensored* on Spike, and these days, *MMA Noise* on LoudernoiseTV—a YouTube channel run by music impresario Allen Kovac.

Through those years and shows I've interviewed hundreds of fighters, but what I saw that night in Rousey was something different, particularly in contrast to her polite and extremely accommodating opponent Miesha "Cupcake" Tate.

Ronda was raw emotion. She wore her heart on her sleeve. She outright cried. She glared. She clenched her teeth. And she's a spectacular athlete and an even more spectacular fighter. A former U.S. judo world champion and Olympic medalist (the first American woman to ever medal in judo at the Olympics), Rousey is several levels above not only her competition, but many of the men in professional mixed martial arts.

Just as abruptly as the woman from the gym left, she re-entered the gym with a drug store bag in tow, and made a beeline to the locker room. Ronda had sent her out to get makeup, hairspray, and a hairbrush. She really had no idea I was going to be there.

When the Baddest Woman on the Planet emerged, she looked way more glamorous than she had a mere 30 minutes ago when she was rag-dolling men on the mat, but her intimidating and now-famous glare was still there.

She walked straight up to me and got right in my face.

"Mike, I don't care who you are or if you're even related to Rupert Murdoch," she said. "But if you ever show up to one of my camps

Rousey, sporting the patented Ronda Rousey glare, enters the arena for a UFC 170 title fight against Sara McMann on February 22, 2014.

UFC president Dana White and Ronda Rousey arrive at The Ultimate Fighter Season Premiere party on September 9, 2014 in Los Angeles, California.

like this ever again, I will never talk to you again. Okay?"

Now, I have been around athletes in camp before, so I didn't take any of this personally. I stood in front of her and said two words, and I meant them.

"I'm sorry."

"Okay, let's do this," was Rousey's response, and with that the crew jumped into action.

The interview was incredible, and after the piece aired on Spike TV, the contrast between Tate and Rousey was so apparent that my co-hosts and I openly feared for Tate's life. We never did air the part about Rupert Murdoch, but that's likely a good thing.

A few weeks later in Columbus, Ohio, I was backstage and did a post-fight interview with the new women's bantamweight champion of the world, "Rowdy" Ronda Rousey, after she won the Strikeforce title from Miesha via a first round armbar that saw Tate's elbow excruciatingly bent and

hyperextended well beyond what any limb should endure.

I approached her with an outstretched hand, being as formal as possible considering our last meeting. She smiled a genuine smile, and said, "Get the hell out of here with that hand, give me a hug." I fell into her arms with relief.

That's Ronda Rousey, at once intimidating and caring. She is a living dichotomy.

People use clichés to describe extraordinary people: best of the best, a woman among girls, in a league of her own, et cetera, et cetera. The irony is, there is nothing cliché about Ronda Rousey, no matter how true those phrases are of her. She is unique in every way—she's a physical specimen with the heart of a lion. Okay, so I'm not above cliché, but then again, isn't that what they're made for?

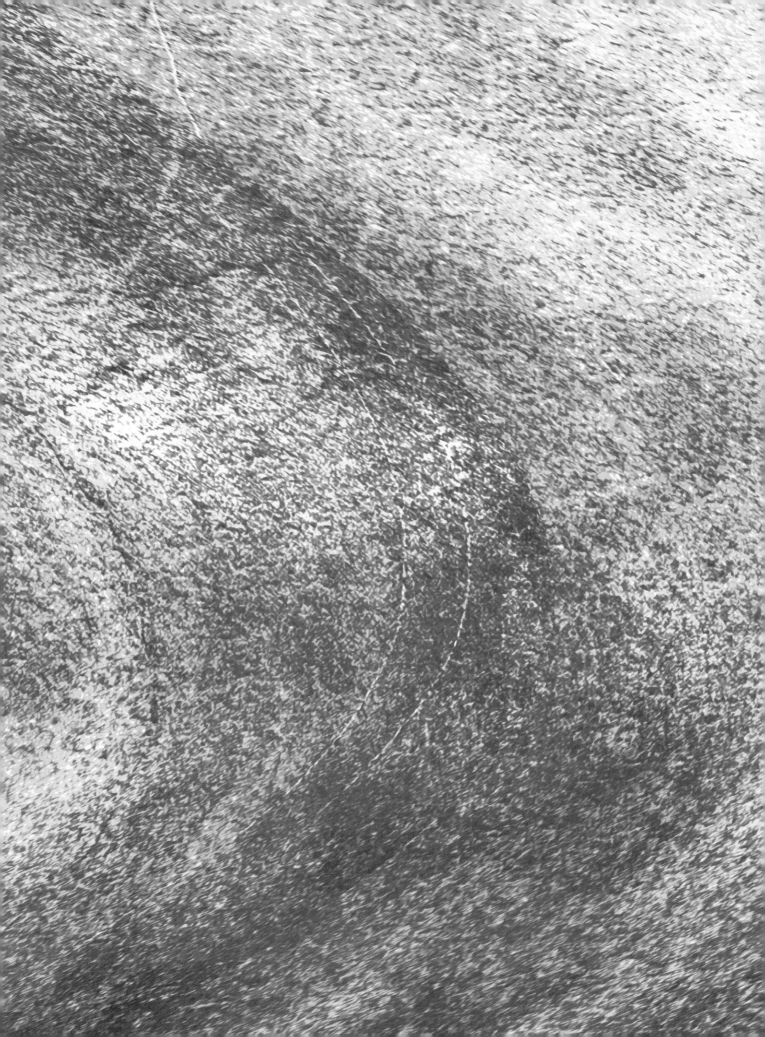

chapter one

The Champ Is Here

> **"I'm not in this world to live up to your expectations, and you're not in this world to live up to mine."**
>
> **—Bruce Lee**

Ronda Rousey is an undefeated mixed martial arts fighter competing in the UFC women's bantamweight division and a former Olympic judoka, taking home bronze for the United States in 2008 at the Beijing Games.

By the time Rousey got to the UFC, she was already the Strikeforce women's bantamweight champion, and her reputation for incredible athleticism and quick stoppages of opponents preceded her.

Mixed martial arts fans don't watch to see *how* Ronda will win, they watch to see *how fast* she will win.

As of this writing, Rousey had 12 professional fights and has only gone past the first round once, in a rematch with Miesha Tate in December of 2013. She won that fight via armbar submission at 54 seconds of the third round. Rousey's last three title defenses are the most impressive times in UFC title fight history, clocking in at 14 seconds (Alexis Davis), 16 seconds (Cat Zingano), and 34 seconds (Bethe Correia) respectively.

A devastating submission specialist, Rousey has a patented armbar that she has perfected after more than two decades of elite judo training. "The Arm Collector" is another popular nickname for the professional MMA fighter, but she co-opted her "Rowdy" nickname

Rousey promoting UFC 190 at Sheraton Rio Hotel & Resort in Copacabana on July 30, 2015.

Ronda dons her favorite boots to walk out to the cage for the Strikeforce Challengers 4 on August 12, 2011. Rousey would win the bout against Sarah D'Alelio with a tapout in the first round.

from the late professional wrestler "Rowdy" Roddy Piper. She even dedicated her 12th win and sixth title defense to Piper, who died suddenly one day before her title fight against Bethe Correia in Rio de Janeiro, Brazil.

In 2014, she won the ESPY for Best Female Athlete and in 2015 received the ESPY for Best Fighter, beating out the vaunted Floyd Mayweather, Jr. for the honor. *Sports Illustrated* has named her Most Dominant Athlete, *New Yorker* magazine calls her the "most bankable star in MMA," and even rapper Eminem is a fan, calling her "slaughterhouse in a blouse" in his song "Shady XV."

She has been featured on the cover of *ESPN the Magazine*'s Body Issue and in *Maxim*, with the caption "Badass & Blonde." She's also appeared in *The Expendables 3*, *Furious 7*, and the *Entourage* movie.

There are only a handful of successful MMA crossover stars, and for the majority of them, it took several more years to cross over than it did Rousey. Fighters who have starred in movies or episodic television, like Chuck Liddell, Gina Carano, Randy Couture, Cung Le, and recently Josh Thomson, have all been around the professional fight game a lot longer than Rousey, but none of them would begrudge her quick ascent to mainstream stardom.

She's earned it.

In 2012, the celebrity news website TMZ caught up with UFC president Dana White outside the famous Mr. Chow's restaurant in Beverly Hills. TMZ asked White when he would have women fighting in the UFC, and he responded, "Never."

White never said that women were not worthy or good enough to compete in the UFC—instead, his position was that there wasn't enough depth in the women's divisions to sustain fan interest.

BITTON
Reebok
Team Haya
Gene & Gok
RESULTS
FITNESS
Reebok
UFC
UFC
UFC

LEFT: Ronda Rousey gets ready to fight Cat Zingano in a UFC 184 title bout on February 28, 2015, in Los Angeles, California. Rousey won after Zingano tapped out 14 seconds into the first round. **TOP:** Rousey laughs after she beat Zingano in just 14 seconds, seemingly in disbelief at how fast that just happened.

UFC champions Frankie Edgar, Ronda Rousey and Chris Weidman appear at a press conference where Reebok announced a new partnership with UFC.

And then Ronda won the belt, and White had little choice but to recant his stance. It was as if Rousey willed him to do it all on her own, and to hear him tell it, she did.

"Ronda Rousey converted me," White told Breitbart Sports. "In the beginning I was trying to sell men fighting on TV, which was tough. Now we're going to try to sell women?"

It's an understandable dilemma to be sure. After all, New York still hasn't sanctioned professional MMA, the lone holdout state in the country. Imagine that! Madison Square Garden is the most famous fighting arena in the world, and Ronda Rousey can't fight there. That's got to be the saddest line in sports journalism ever written.

Luckily for White, Rousey does a pretty good job of not only selling herself, but selling women's fighting, period. While being called the "most dominant athlete in any sport" is nice

Ronda with Michael Strahan and her mom AnnMaria De Mars attend the UFC on Fox event at Staples Center in 2012.

and all, leaving a legacy, and literally building an industry for women competitors in mixed martial arts, is something Rousey has set her mind to as she looks to her future after fighting.

That's not to say there's no place for women fighters outside of the UFC. World Series of Fighting, Bellator, and Invicta FC are all viable options for professional women's MMA—if not feeder leagues for the UFC—but what Rousey has done for women fighters goes well beyond livelihoods. More importantly, when girls look at their parents and say they want to be a mixed martial arts competitor, they may find them not so steadfast against the notion.

Rousey has made fighting acceptable for women.

She has proved to the most ardent critics of MMA (not even just *women's* MMA) that fighting is a technical skill acquired only after years of rigorous training.

On August 6, 2010, Ronda tried mixed martial arts for the first time.

It was an amateur event in Oxnard, California, in Combat Fight League's Ground Zero event. Rousey wasn't too sure what to expect, or even if her judo training would help in the fight, but she was determined to win. Little did she know she had zero cause to doubt herself. In just 23 seconds, Ronda had her answer. Her opponent Hayden Munoz threw a left kick to Ronda's right thigh. Ronda caught the kick, and attacked for a takedown. She quickly got on top of Munoz and maneuvered for an armbar. Munoz tapped (a tap is a signal that the fighter concedes victory to one's opponent), and that was that.

Rousey began training her striking (stand-up fighting) under renowned coach Edmond Tarverdyan at Glendale Fighting Club shortly before turning professional, and in her first pro bout her coach told her to use her judo to win. It wasn't that Edmond wasn't

Ronda gets ready for her UFC 157 women's bantamweight championship match with Liz Carmouche on February 23, 2013.

Ronda takes down judo coach Justin Flores at Glendale Fighting Club in July 2015.

Miesha Tate gets her elbow hyperextended by a Rousey armbar during the UFC 168 fight on December 28, 2013 in Las Vegas, Nevada. Rousey won by a third round tap out.

Rousey and Carmouche during their UFC women's world bantamweight championship bout. Ronda proves she has the heart of a champion when she overcomes a nasty neck crank that dislocated her jaw against Carmouche.

confident in Ronda's striking, it was more a lesson in "if it ain't broke, don't fix it."

That fight took place in the King of the Cage promotion on March 27, 2011, in Tarzana, California. Ronda submitted her opponent in 25 seconds this time, with another armbar. In her first 11 fights as an amateur and a pro, Rousey used an armbar to

UFC President Dana White looks on as Rousey and challenger Holly Holm face-off at the MGM Grand Garden Arena to promote their November 2015 fight, UFC 193.

submit all of her opponents, all in the first round, eight of them in under a minute.

Word of Rousey's dominance spread like wildfire among MMA fans.

Mixed martial arts is the first international sport born in the Internet era, and it was the Internet that kept it alive, even as legislators had it banned in the 1990s. That story has been well

Ronda Rousey smiles during a workout at Glendale Fighting Club.

Ronda poses with her UFC belt on December 2, 2014 in New York City.

documented, but when Zuffa (Lorenzo and Frank Fertitta, Dana White) bought the UFC, the sport was pretty much an underground obsession. It took tens of millions of dollars and then, even after being $40 million in the red, they still funded *The Ultimate Fighter* on Spike TV, which was a time buy (meaning Zuffa not only paid for the production but also the air time). It was a fight between Forrest Griffin and Stephan Bonnar, live on Spike TV in 2006, that is widely credited for saving the UFC and the sport of mixed martial arts, as millions of people watched the fight, with more and more tuning in as the two went to war on national television. People were calling their friends, imploring them to tune into Spike TV to watch something incredible happening.

Little did they know that less than 10 years later, another fighter—and a woman at that—would be the one to usher the sport into the pop culture zeitgeist. ∎

Ronda celebrates appearing on the cover of *ESPN the Magazine*'s annual Body Issue.

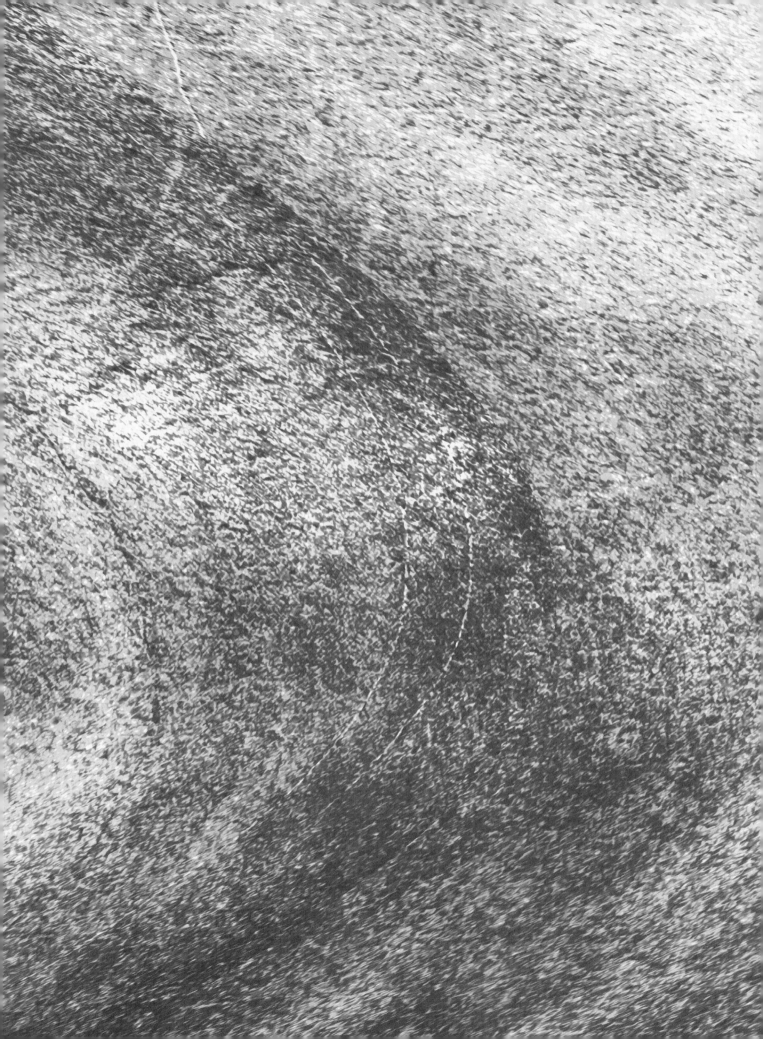

chapter two
Unfinished Business

> **"The easiest thing to do in the world is pull the covers up over your head and go back to sleep."**
>
> —Dan Gable

Ronda began training judo under her mother, Dr. AnnMaria De Mars, at age 11. In 1984, De Mars became the first American (man or woman) to win a world championship in judo. (Ronda would take silver in the 2007 World Judo Championships.)

There were several nights during Ronda's childhood when she would be awoken to an ambush from her mother, forcing her to execute an armbar out of a deep sleep.

It's no wonder that today, Rowdy Ronda can find her way to a fight-ending armbar in every situation inside the Octagon.

In 2003 during a practice, Ronda tore her ACL and required surgery a few months before the judo Senior Open,

an important tournament being held in Las Vegas that year. It was supposed to be Ronda's debutante party in the judo community. Rousey—being a teenager—moped around for about a week before her mother had had enough of watching her spawn sitting on the couch watching TV, feeling sorry for herself.

"It's been a week," Ronda wrote her mom saying in her best-selling autobiography *My Fight/Your Fight* (Regan Arts, 2015). Ronda protested that the surgeon told her not to train too soon after surgery. "What about your other leg?" said De Mars. "What about your abs? Last time I checked sit-ups didn't involve knees."

AnnMaria De Mars told Ronda not to take too long with Bethe Correia.
After the 34-second competition, Rousey celebrates her victory over
Correia (not pictured).

Ronda's mother is tough as nails. The apple didn't fall too far from that tree, but no matter how tough Ronda is, her mother is and always will be the alpha.

For example, when Ronda took offense to Brazilian fighter Bethe Correia's poorly worded trash talk leading up to their UFC 190 title fight, saying she hoped "Ronda doesn't kill

Following Bethe Correia's defeat during UFC 190, Rousey flashes her "happy dance" smile when Big John McCarthy raises her hand.

herself" after Correia beats her, Ronda said she would prolong the fight in order to punish her. Dr. De Mars told Ronda that was one of the stupidest things she's ever heard.

Ronda won that fight by way of knockout in just 34 seconds.

From the very start of her judo career, Rousey was determined to be accepted into a world dominated by dominant men. Most of her early training partners were men. Her coaches were men. Her mother was preparing her for a tough road.

When she turned 16, Ronda's mother sent her to renowned judo coach "Big Jim" Pedro's academy in Massachusetts, so that she could train with some of the world's best players, including his son, Jimmy Pedro, Jr., a multiple world champion and US Olympic team captain and two-time bronze medalist.

It was a lonely time for Rousey. She stayed in rural Massachusetts for much of her tenure there, living in a spare bedroom in Big Jim's isolated house. Her coach was also a firefighter, and he was rarely there. Also during this time, Rousey began a grueling international tournament schedule that saw her travel the world over the next five years.

Anyone who travels a lot for a living knows how grueling it can be. Sure, you're visiting new cities and getting to experience parts of the world that you would probably never get to see, but try doing it while cutting weight and training and then fighting a world class athlete.

During this time, Ronda's training was absolutely rigorous. When it comes to elite level, world class athletes, the club is exclusive and the love comes tough. If Rousey thought her mother was tough on her while growing up, she was just an appetizer to the main course of training for the Olympics.

Rousey was in constant proving-herself mode. No matter how hard she worked, it wasn't hard enough. If she cried, she was mocked. When she improvised judo technique, she was criticized. It was a world filled with tradition. It was their way or the highway, and Ronda took the highway several times, sometimes having to live in her car. She was thrown out of friends' homes, forced to sleep in a crowded living room with someone's feet in her face—you name it, she went through it while on the glamorous road to so-called judo fame. Ronda did her best to walk their line, but the truth is: Can you name one world famous judo player not mentioned in the last few pages? Exactly. Theirs was not Ronda's path to take, and luckily she had the fortitude and the audacity not only to take a different path, but to pave her own with her blood, sweat, and tears.

Luckily for every MMA fan in the world, and for so many girls, boys, men, and women who have been inspired by her phenomenal talent and indomitable strength, things didn't play out in judo the way she had hoped they would.

Thank God she lost.

Rousey was and still is a judo phenom. By the time she was 15 years old, she was beating players who were twice her age. In 2004 at the Junior World Championships in Budapest, Ronda defeated China's Jing Jing Mao with a slam takedown in just four seconds. It was a prelude to what would come in her MMA career, where thus far, her average fight lasts just over a minute.

That same year, at age 17, Rousey made the US Olympic judo team as the youngest judoka in the games, though she failed to medal. She was devastated. While most others would live out their first Olympic experience (the host city was Athens, after all, the birthplace of the games), Rousey took the first available flight home after the loss, re-living her match over and over

Ronda Rousey during the weigh-ins for UFC 190. After hiring Mike Dolce to help her hit 135 pounds, Rousey no longer struggled to make weight.

Bronze medalist Ronda Rousey is the first American woman to medal in Olympic judo competition.

again during the 16-plus hour flight home to Los Angeles.

Even at 17 years old, there was nobody harder on Ronda Rousey than Ronda Rousey.

In 2008 in Beijing, China, during the Summer Olympic Games, Ronda became the first woman in US judo history to win a medal. For most mere mortals, any Olympic medal would have been satisfactory, but for Rousey, it was utter failure.

They say combat sports players remember their losses more than they remember their wins. It haunts them, even as they achieve greatness in the future. But that doesn't mean they want to go back to avenge them.

The day after Rousey won the Strikeforce bantamweight championship belt in March 2012, Ronda made appearances at the annual Arnold Classic bodybuilding contest and expo inside the Columbus Convention Center in Ohio. I met the new champion at the Gaspari Nutrition booth for a lengthy sit-down interview (Rich Gaspari, the multiple-time bodybuilding champion who owns the eponymous supplement company, was one of Rousey's sponsors). You may recall her wearing the Gaspari Nutrition logo on the front of her sports bra during most of her early pro fights.

I asked her if coming up short in the Olympics had given her the extra drive to be successful in mixed martial arts.

"I have all my fire taking care of this belt right now," she said, holding on to her brand new gold and gem–encrusted belt in the Gaspari booth. "I can't be happy doing judo right now. People change careers several time in their lives, and this is what I'm meant to do now. I'm going to go to the Olympics and support my teammates and I'm going to cheer them on and hope someone else can win the gold this time around. My work is done in that sport."

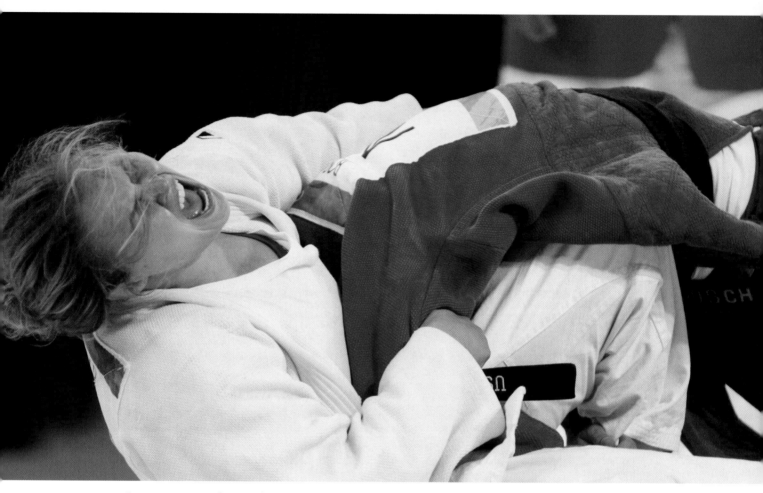

Ronda Rousey gives it her all against Edith Bosch of the Netherlands in the preliminaries at the Beijing 2008 Olympics.

That very well may be, but so many of today's greatest MMA fighters have some unfinished business they need to deal with.

UFC light heavyweight champion Daniel Cormier was captain of the 2008 USA Olympic wrestling team but didn't compete after suffering kidney failure during his weight cut. UFC Hall of Famer Randy Couture failed to make the USA Greco-Roman team (he was an alternate but didn't get to compete). Despite being an NCAA Division-1 All-American wrestler, former UFC lightweight champion— and one of the sport's pound for pound best—Frankie Edgar lost a final college wrestling match in triple overtime and missed being named an All-American. These highly competitive athletes all have unfinished business in their competitive lives that drives them to keep competing.

They've all left something on the mat.

I pushed the theory that losing Olympic gold is what drives her to utterly demolish her competition.

"Absolutely," she said. "I believe that everything happens for a reason. I trained so hard for the Olympics and when I got the bronze I was kind of wondering why that happened. I think the reason why is that I would still have this drive and try to achieve more. If I got the gold medal in judo I think I might have retired myself mentally, and thought I did what I needed to do and not gone on to this [MMA]. Yeah, I think you're totally right, you need to have some unfinished business."

Judo competitor Ronda Rousey poses in her USA Team sweats for a portrait during the USOC Media Summit Chicago on April 14, 2008.

Ronda trains with her adoring fans
watching at Pepe beach in Barra da
Tijuca, Brazil, in July 2015.

After coming home with a bronze medal, and just $10,000 for her effort, Rousey was pretty much broke. There is only so much sponsorship money to go around when it comes to supporting Olympic athletes, and most sponsors only care about the high visibility sports.

Judo is not one of them.

Ronda worked three jobs to make ends meet. She was teaching judo at a friend's dojo, working the overnight shift at a gym, and was a bartender at a bar in Long Beach, California.

She was living in a tiny studio apartment with bad plumbing, and often times came home to a house with sewage coming out of her toilet and shower. If things weren't bad enough already, her boyfriend, an ex-heroin addict, relapsed and stole her car.

Ronda wasn't too much of a fan of mixed martial arts, but used to catch fights with her guy friends from judo every once in a while.

The first women's fight she saw featured a bout between former Strikeforce champion turned movie actress Gina Carano (her father, Glenn Carano, was an NFL quarterback) and Julie Kedzie. The fight was a competitive stand-up war that impressed Rousey, but she gave little thought to pursuing a career in MMA.

That is, until she realized life after Olympic glory wasn't all that she had hoped it would be.

One night at the bar, a women's MMA fight played on one of the flatscreens that hung over the bar. Rousey, who by now had a recreational drug habit that included prescription painkillers, pot, and vodka, looked up and said to no one in particular, "I can totally do that."

With few career prospects, Rousey eased up on the partying, went back to the gym, and mixed martial arts was in for a perfect storm of looks, skill, determination, and charisma the likes of which the industry has never seen before. ■

Rousey is pulled off Correia by Big John McCarthy following their August 1, 2015 fight at HSBC Arena.

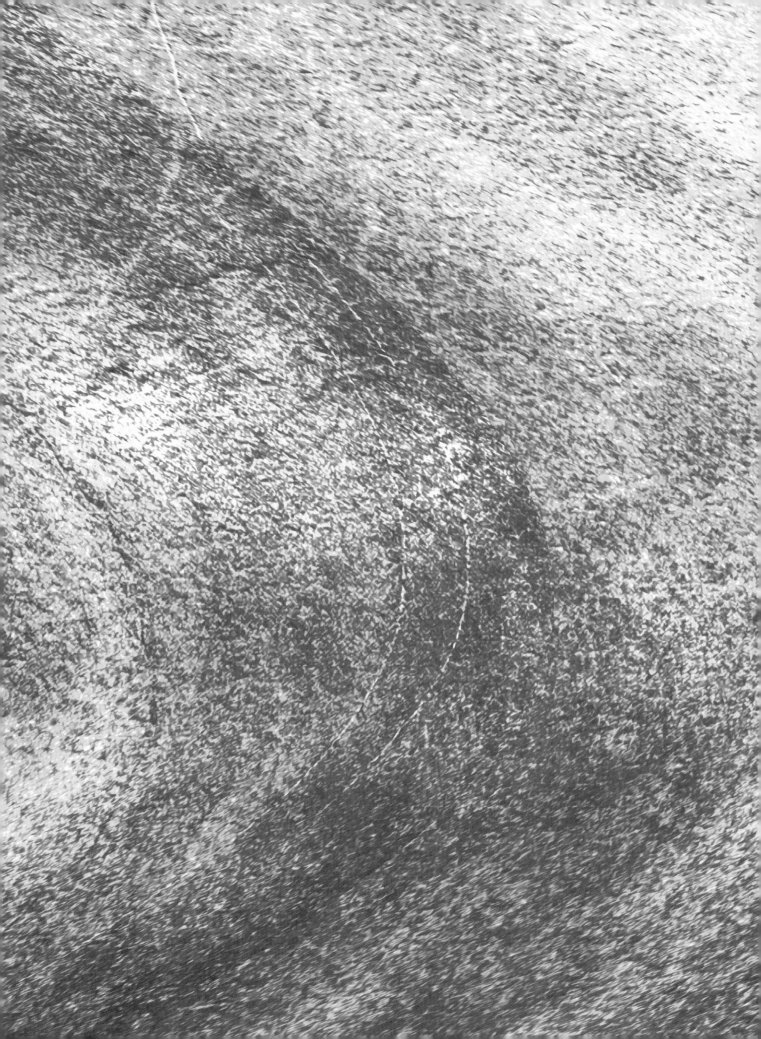

chapter three

Growing Up Rousey

> # "Children are likely to live up to what you believe of them."
> ## —Lady Bird Johnson

Ronda Jean Rousey was born on February 1, 1987, with the umbilical cord wrapped around her neck. She was blue. It's fitting and a bit ironic that she makes her living 28 years later in a sport where choking someone out or being choked out is the norm. The doctors and nurses worked frantically to bring her back to life, and when they did they were concerned that she would have some brain damage due to the trauma.

The brain damage took form as a speech impediment that Ronda has struggled with most of her life. It was only after she described her symptoms in her autobiography that she discovered—through a fan with a daughter suffering the same symptoms—that she most likely had Developmental Apraxia, or Childhood Apraxia of Speech. Children who have the condition can understand speech and know exactly what they want to say, but are unable to form the words with their mouth and tongue.

Ronda was six years old before she would complete an understandable sentence. She has literally fought for everything in her life.

Ronda is named after her father, Ron Rousey, and to Ronda, he was the strongest man in the world. The family moved from California to North Dakota after Ronda's older sister Jennifer witnessed a man getting shot while walking home from school. It was in North Dakota that her father broke his back while sledding down a hill, a freak injury that eventually led to him taking his own life. Ronda was just eight years old when he died.

Rousey gets physically and mentally ready to fight.

Ronda Rousey fights Brazil's Mayra Aguiar da Silva at the Pan American Games in Rio de Janeiro on July 20, 2007. Rousey took home the gold medal.

"None of us were ever the same after that," Rousey wrote in her autobiography.

That tragic event has been a constant influence in Rousey's life and it is what drives her more than anything else in her professional career. It's as if Ronda is constantly fighting for the approval of her father, or at the very least, avenging him in every fight.

After all, it was Ronald Rousey who told his daughter that she would be a world class athlete, and that she would shine on the world stage. And it was her mother who demanded the very best from her daughters, at all times. If the

Lady Bird Johnson quote at the top of this chapter ever needed qualification, see Ronda Rousey.

Understandably, the face of women's mixed martial arts does not like talking about her father in interviews, and said as much in a 2013 FOX television special.

"I feel like I'm prostituting his memory for my own career gain," she said, through tears.

When Ronda was 11 she found a scrapbook that highlighted her mother's judo career, and it proved to be an unexpected revelation for the impressionable girl. For years, Rousey

From left, silver medalist Anaysi Hernández of Cuba, gold medalist Masae Ueno of Japan, bronze medalist USA's Ronda Rousey, and bronze medalist Edith Bosch of the Netherlands hold their medals during the 2008 Olympics in Beijing.

Ronda Rousey attends the Fox Sports Media Upfront party on March 5, 2013 in New York.

thought that it was her father who was the tough one, when little did she know, her mom was just as, or even more tough.

Dr. AnnMaria De Mars does not suffer fools, especially when it's her own daughter who is acting like one. When Ronda tore her ACL in judo class, her trainer had to convince De Mars to take her to the hospital. When Ronda broke her toe, De Mars told her to run laps. The lessons she was teaching was that even through injury, you could still perform, and it has paid dividends for Rousey. In many judo matches and in at least one UFC fight, Rousey has been in uncomfortable situations that have tested her resolve, and she's always passed with flying colors.

Ronda dropped out of high school to pursue her amateur judo career (she got her GED years later). She traveled the world, not only competing, but also training with the best judokas

in the world. Most of her friends were men—not just men, but some of the toughest men on the planet. Ronda was constantly working harder than everybody else, just to prove she belonged.

On Steve Austin's podcast in August 2015, former UFC middleweight star Chael Sonnen attributed much of Ronda's professional fighting success not so much to skill, but to experience.

"She's been at it her whole life through the judo circuit," he said. "She's been to two different Olympic games. She's shaken hands with another girl, competed with the lights on, and found a way to get her hand raised. Those other girls don't have that. The division is brand new. It's maybe three years old. They don't have the amateur backgrounds, the professional backgrounds or anything that's extensive. They're not great competitors. That's what separates Ronda. It's more of an intangible than

A young Ronda Rousey fields questions during a news conference of the US judo team prior to the 2004 Olympics in Athens.

they never walked in her shoes. For men, whether they be judo players, tae kwon do fighters, wrestlers, or jiu-jitsu grapplers, traveling with gear and sleeping on floors a few inches from your teammates in a sweaty basement in some rural town is pretty much the acceptable way of life, but try doing it as a 16-year-old girl, and the dynamics are very different. Try doing it as the only girl, in most cases, in the gym.

Ronda spent a lot of time crying. She cried during and after practice. She cried alone in her room. She cried during competition. And whether she won or lost, she cried after. At 16 years old, Rousey was ranked No. 1 in the world in her weight division, but even as her confidence in her judo game grew, her self-esteem shrank amidst the constant struggle to make weight. For years, Ronda fought at 139 pounds, and the more she trained, the more muscle weight she put on, which is notoriously harder to cut than fat or water.

physical. She's a competitor and these other girls aren't."

But earning that kind of practical experience didn't come easy to Rousey.

Many people in the judo community regarded Ronda as a spoiled brat—but

Cutting weight just a little over 10 years ago is much different than cutting weight is today. There were no nutritionists specializing in helping athletes make weight like there are today with carefully measured flax seed and perfectly portioned chicken breast with a side of exactly two ounces of fresh spinach.

Iconic boxer Mike Tyson visits Rousey during an open workout session.

Instead, athletes starved themselves, ran in plastic suits under layers of sweatsuits, jumped ropes in saunas and spit in cups. At the elite level, there is no excuse not to make weight, and instead of helping those who struggle with it, teammates and coaches usually ridicule. Anyone who misses weight is immediately labeled as lazy or selfish. Ronda was so obsessed with her weight that she became bulimic.

During this time, Rousey had serious body image issues. She regarded her frame as thick and stocky, and it didn't help that her boyfriend, a judo player several years older than she at the time, called her "maybe a six" on a scale of one to ten, and would point out women he thought were hot—usually very thin girls. Rousey, with her strong shoulders and powerful thighs, couldn't compete with that image, so she forced herself to throw up after meals.

"I made myself throw up because I associated the feeling of full with guilt," she has said in interviews.

It would take her a few years to get over her bulimia. In fact, it wasn't until she was on a European judo tournament circuit and ended up in the wrong city for a match that she finally got over her battle with weight. She was in Vienna for a tournament and didn't know it was moved to Helsinki. Devastated, she called her mother in tears, saying she was going to come home. Her mother told her to get on a train, and just compete at the next weight class up. She did. And she won. It was at that moment when Ronda realized that she was in control of her destiny, not USA Judo, not her trainers and not her teammates.

It was all up to her, and it was an empowering feeling.

Her father's death was certainly a formative moment in her life. Discovering that her mother was a judo

Ronda throws Annett Boehm to win the bronze at the Beijing 2008 Olympics on August 13, 2008.

Rousey is overcome with emotion after beating Annett Boehm of Germany at the women's judo -70kg middleweight division finals at the Beijing 2008 Olympics.

champion and choosing to try out De Mars' sport was the next monumental moment, but the realization that she was in control of her own destiny might be the seismic shift that turned Ronda into the worldwide phenomenon she is today.

Today, after appearing in *Maxim* and *Sports Illustrated* and *ESPN the Magazine*, Rousey is seen as a sex symbol. But while her body has always been a specimen, she struggled with her appearance during her formative years. She used to hide her biceps, because her peers would tell her she had the physique of a boy, but those biceps would prove useful several years later when she met with Sylvester Stallone about a part in the movie *The Expendables 3*.

"Those biceps," Stallone told her, "they're awesome." When Ronda showed up to the set on her first day of filming, her wardrobe was different than what she had been fitted for. "Sly said your biceps are beautiful," the stylist told her. "He wants people to see them."

Incidentally, about that *Maxim* shoot. Rousey purposely arrived to the shoot weighing 16 pounds more than her fighting weight of 135 pounds. She didn't want girls to think they need to look like someone who works three months through rigorous training and dieting to look the way she does during fight week.

And she was still a 10, if you ask me. ■

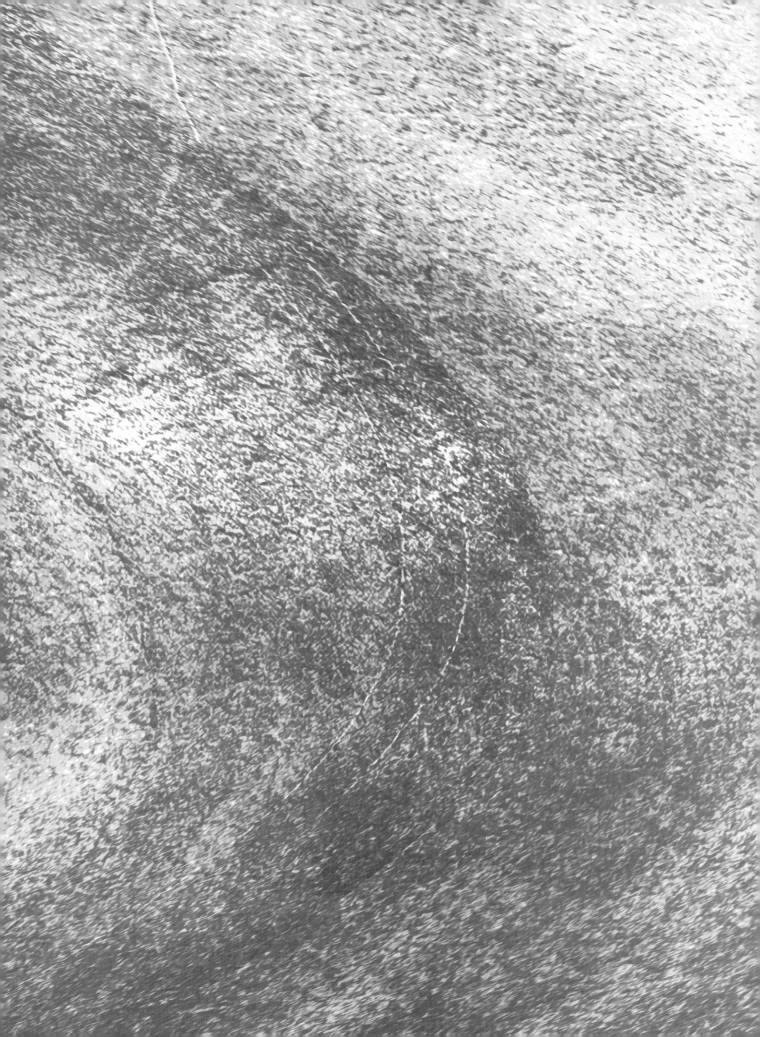

chapter four

Building Women's MMA

> **"The question isn't who isn't going to let me. It's who is going to stop me."**
>
> **—Ayn Rand**

Ronda Rousey ascended the world of mixed martial arts rapidly. In the beginning, it was just the world of women's MMA, but today, she is unquestionably the sport's biggest star. Before her came names like Renzo Gracie, B.J. Penn, Chuck Liddell, Tito Ortiz, Anderson Silva, Randy Couture, Chael Sonnen, Frankie Edgar, Urijah Faber, and Gina Carano. Ronda, in a shorter amount of time, has climbed to the top, not only regarding popularity, but also in monetary terms.

While the UFC is a private company and most of its financial dealings are never really disclosed, a prize fighter's show and win purse has to be announced to the state athletic commission, and since they are a public entity, that information is available.

For UFC 190 (although this fight took place in Brazil), Rousey's disclosed income for the fight was $230,000, which included $70,000 to show, $70,000 to win, a $50,000 Performance of the Night bonus, and a $40,000 Reebok sponsorship. That does not include a piece of the pay-per-view. Once again, those numbers are also private, but there have been reports that the event sold over 900,000 PPVs. Now, I've heard from some high-level fighters that a piece of the PPV can be anywhere between $1 to $8, and it's structured on a tier, where the lower the number of buys, the lower the piece, but as the buys get higher, so does a fighter's participation percentage. Suffice it to say, Ronda pulled in well over $1 million for her 12th title defense,

Ronda reverses Cat Zingano in mid-air during a UFC 184 title bout in Los Angeles, California.

Ronda Rousey (right) maneuvers for the armbar against Cat Zingano.

and that doesn't include commercial endorsements and other sponsorships, like Metro-PCS and Represent Clothing, where Ronda serves as spokesperson.

Note that I am not privy to any inside information, and anything above is speculative, but I am an educated guesser.

When Ronda was signed on to Strikeforce, she only fought twice before being granted a title shot. Many of the women on the roster, including the champion Miesha Tate, thought Rousey was being gifted a title shot. The rank-and-file women agreed. Here again, Rousey was being depicted as a spoiled brat. Like in judo, she was regarded as the heel (in professional wrestling parlance).

But her first two Strikeforce fights lasted a combined one minute, six seconds, and the fans were clamoring for a title match. If there's one thing Dana White is good at, it's giving fans what they want.

Ronda beat Tate with a first round armbar that was hard to watch. Tate's elbow was hyperextended and it looked downright ugly. That said, Tate showed unbelievable toughness, and refused to tap even as her elbow snapped, crackled, and popped with every thrust of Ronda's hips. When an armbar is applied correctly, the elbow is placed between the legs of the person applying it, and while thrusting one's hip upwards, the applicant will pull down on the forearm and wrist, thus ripping tendons and muscle if one doesn't tap out in time. Miesha didn't tap for several seconds, allowing Rousey to do significant damage to her elbow before

Ronda locks in the fight-ending armbar against Carmouche in her UFC debut to defend her belt for the first time.

In the gym where she was once ignored, Rousey's nickname "Rowdy" now adorns most of the heavy bags.

finally conceding at 4:27 of the first round.

Ronda would defend her belt just once in Strikeforce before White decided he would build the women's UFC division around Rousey.

She fought a very game Sarah Kaufman on August 18, 2012, at the Valley View Casino Center in San Diego, California. Kaufman last won on the same card in which Ronda took the belt from Tate, in an impressive bout vs. Alexis Davis. She won by majority decision in a war that will go down as one of the best fights in women's MMA history.

At the time, many fans and fighters believed that Kaufman should have been the one fighting for the belt instead of participating in a title eliminator bout, but she became the No. 1 contender that night, and the first test of Rousey's reign at the top.

Rousey submitted Kaufman in 54 seconds.

Rousey's UFC debut was a big moment in mixed martial arts history. There was a lot of speculation about this "experiment" known as women's MMA. Even White himself was skeptical that there would be enough talent in the division, and he made sure that there was a compelling line-up of fights leading up to the main event of UFC 157 on February 23, 2013, which featured Rousey, the newly minted UFC bantamweight champion, against former US Marine Liz Carmouche.

The main card featured legends like Urijah Faber, Dan Henderson, Lyoto Machida, and future welterweight champion Robbie Lawler.

There were some 15,525 tickets sold for a live gate of $1.4 million, and a reported 500,000 pay-per-view sales.

Carmouche took Rousey's back early in the fight and, while Ronda stood up in the middle of the cage, began looking for a rear-naked choke. Ronda kept her chin tucked so Carmouche switched

TOP: Rousey and Bethe Correia face off during weigh-ins for UFC 190 at HSBC Arena. **RIGHT:** Rousey celebrates after defeating Correia with a left hook during the UFC 190 match in Rio de Janeiro on August 1, 2015.

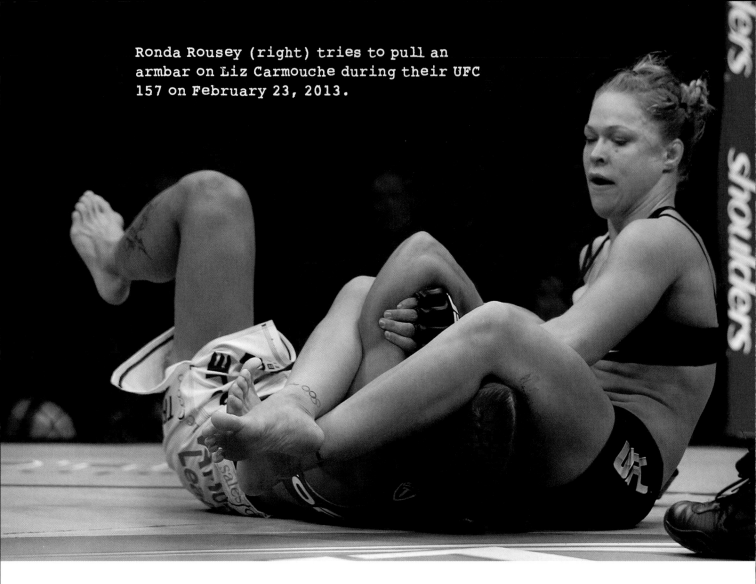

Ronda Rousey (right) tries to pull an armbar on Liz Carmouche during their UFC 157 on February 23, 2013.

to a nasty neck crank. This is a very painful move, and coming from a former Marine it could not have felt very good.

Ronda said she felt her jaw dislocate, and her teeth were digging in into the back of her lips. Liz was pulling on Ronda's neck so hard she could have broken it. Rousey, however, kept her cool. She remembered to stay in the middle of the cage, so that Liz couldn't rest her back against the fence while on

Rousey's back, and she worked to get Carmouche's legs apart. When she did, she slipped Carmouche off her back and went on to win the match with a series of ground-and-pound blows and then, of course, the armbar.

After the fight, Carmouche was asked if she thought she had the fight won.

"Neck cranks are hard to pull off," she said with her ever present smile and good nature. "If she has heart she can pull through like she did. She was successful. I beared down and I have teeth marks on my arm and I was thinking maybe I can get her to tap out by knocking some teeth out but it didn't quite work out."

Dana White said the fight was awesome. "Anyone who has ever rolled before knows when someone takes your back and puts that on your face, on your jaw and on your teeth that is no fun. I don't think Ronda will be eating a lot of food at her after-party tonight," he said.

Ronda was about 20 minutes late to the news conference and it is telling that in her first answer she looked over to Carmouche and apologized for her teeth going into her arm. She explained that when she was a kid she had dislocated her jaw and that the injury still causes some problems.

"Sorry, it was not intentional at all, dude," she said. They both laughed.

When asked how she felt when Carmouche was cranking her neck, Ronda said she wasn't worried but was very aware of the severity of the moment.

As for the main event and delivering a great fight, Ronda said she was "honored to be part of it. It might take a while to sink in."

In a telling moment during the press conference, Ronda showed that her newfound celebrity was something she was dealing with from a healthy and humble perspective. When asked about all of the media attention she said, "I'm going to go off the grid for a week, and when I see anybody I'm not going to talk about me. There will be no talking about me for about a week."

I've seen many fighters go through their share of egotism, but for the most part, mixed martial arts fighters are usually the most grounded of all professional athletes. After all, history has shown that no matter how good

Rousey knocks out
Olympic wrestler
Sara McMann with a
well placed knee to the
midsection during a
UFC 170 title fight on
February 22, 2014.

one is, there will inevitably come a time when you will come face to face with the next big thing, and in this sport, you're only as good as your last fight.

Ronda was scheduled to fight Cat Zingano next. In fact, she was pitted against Zingano in yet another historic moment for the sport, a co-ed edition of *The Ultimate Fighter*.

The Ultimate Fighter is a reality show produced by Craig Piligian of Pilgrim Films. Piligian is one of the pioneers of reality TV. He was one of the original producers on Mark Burnett's *Survivor*. In *The Ultimate Fighter*, two teams of UFC hopefuls share a house in the Las Vegas suburbs, and train to beat the heck out of each other. The winner of the show earns a six-figure UFC contract. Many greats have been featured on the show, and many great fighters got their start on the show.

Fighters like Jessamyn Duke, Kenny Florian, Stephan Bonnar, Forrest Griffin, Rashad Evans, and one of Ronda's judo training partners and oldest friends, Manny Gamburyan, have all come out of the show. Even former UFC welterweight champion Matt Serra was a cast member on a *TUF* season dubbed "The Comeback," which featured fighters who were nearing the end of their careers. Serra won, and then went on to knock out Georges St-Pierre to win the belt in what is widely regarded as the biggest upset in UFC history.

On the first day of shooting, Ronda was greeted by her nemesis, Miesha Tate. At first, Rousey thought Zingano brought Tate in as an assistant coach in order to get into Ronda's head. But it was later revealed that Cat had injured her knee, and Miesha was brought in as a replacement coach whom Ronda would fight at the end of the season.

Ronda Rousey waits on stage for the weigh-in for her UFC women's bantamweight title fight against Miesha Tate.

Rousey did not take the news very well.

Ronda has been criticized about her reaction to the cast change. Again, "spoiled brat" was the term used to describe her. But she tells a backstory in her book that sheds so much more light into her state of mind.

Rousey's manager had been negotiating with Dana White, and Dana wasn't too pleased with one of his negotiating points, and he called Ronda directly. Ronda was not privy to the negotiations (most talent never is), and was a bit upset with her manager. Fast forward to Miesha stepping in to coach for Cat. Ronda actually thought she was being fired and made an example of by White. Knowing what we know now, Ronda's reaction was more than justified.

Ronda fought Miesha for the second time on December 28, 2013. It would be the first time Ronda was taken out of Round 1, but aside from a few very hard shots, Ronda was dominant in every round. She finished Miesha in Round 3 with, what else? An armbar. But it was the first time Ronda displayed the beginning of a solid striking game.

By the time Rousey faced Bethe Correia in August 2015, her striking game had come a long

Ronda Rousey attends an event to promote UFC 190 on July 30, 2015 in Rio de Janeiro.

way. After her fight with Alexis Davis, Rousey underwent hand surgery, and she took the time to apply the same lesson her mother taught her back when she had ACL surgery when she was 15 years old. Instead of sitting around, she developed her left hook, which is what she used to knock Correia unconscious in just 34 seconds.

Sara McMann is a silver medalist in US Olympic wrestling. When she faced Ronda in February 2015, the pundits couldn't help but wonder how Rousey would fare against one who had the same kind of training and work ethic she possessed. After all, making the women's Olympic wrestling team is as grueling and intense as making the judo team.

Would Ronda be able to take Sara down? Would Sara be able to defend Ronda's judo? The answer came in just 66 seconds, when, after McMann did successfully defend a takedown attempt by Rousey, she also ate a knee to the liver, and was rendered indefensible. The referee stepped in and waved the fight off before McMann endured any more damage from the champ.

A knee to the liver is one of the most devastating blows imaginable. It is as debilitating a blow as any. Anthony Pettis scored a technical knockout over Donald "Cowboy" Cerrone with a liver kick. Bas Rutten patented an open hand liver strike while fighting in Rings. And I once took a liver shot—just to see how it feels—from UFC lightweight great Jim Miller. I peed blood for three days (I was also tasered on Neil Cavuto's show on national television—YouTube that clip if you're a hater—you'll get a good laugh).

When Ronda finally did face Cat Zingano, it was one of the most anticipated fights in women's MMA history. Zingano is a Brazilian jiu-jitsu black belt. She's one of the fiercest fighters in the world. She was supposed to be the biggest test of Ronda Rousey's career.

After Cat blew out her knee and underwent surgery, many wondered if she would be able to rebound and be as dominant as she was prior to the surgery, when she had defeated Miesha Tate via TKO by way of a barrage of knees and punches. If a career-threatening injury wasn't enough, Cat's

Ronda Rousey (left) stares down Alexis Davis as they pose for photographers during a weigh-in for the UFC 175 event on July 4, 2014.

husband of seven years committed suicide while Cat was recovering from surgery.

It was yet another in a series of tragedies that has rocked the affable wrestler from Denver, Colorado.

Zingano lost her best friend to murder just before she was set to try out for the US Olympic wrestling team. That same year she lost her mother to brain cancer. At age 23, she became pregnant but her boyfriend left long before

Ronda Rousey shakes Liz Carmouche from her back during their UFC 157 women's bantamweight championship match in Anaheim, California. Rousey won by tapout in the first round.

Brayden was born. Then, just as she was set to take on Rousey, her world came crashing down once again.

Mauricio Zingano owned a Brazilian jiu-jitsu school and offered Cat free lessons. He quickly became her head trainer and husband, and under his coaching she became the No. 1 contender to face Rousey. When she blew out her knee and lost the chance to earn enough money to buy her own home (they were sharing a home with Zingano's ex-wife), Mauricio became despondent. He blamed Cat for getting injured. He became a different person.

After his suicide, Zingano had to be strong for her son. It is simultaneously the greatest and hardest thing one can do for one's child. Mauricio had adopted Brayden and the boy was taking the death as hard as Cat.

"I lost my best friend, my coach, my husband, my home, my car, my income," she told ESPN at the time. "I lost everything. I would be completely

justified sitting on my ass all day, but I want my son to see something else. So he knows he can do it too."

She returned to the Octagon against Amanda Nunes at UFC 178 and won in Round 3 with a series of hammer fists. After her victory, she let out a triumphant roar, something primordial that had deeper meaning than just winning a fight.

She was named Rousey's next opponent.

When Cat heard about Ronda's dad's suicide, she remarked, "Damn, that's why she's so good. She made it through that. If you survive what we have, what's a fight?"

Ronda doesn't hold back anything. Remember when I showed up to her camp? That's nothing compared to the words she reserves for her opponents or other fighters.

On Georges St-Pierre: "I respect Georges St-Pierre as a businessman and an athlete. I don't have anything against him personally. But he's not the kind of fighter I like watching."

On Miesha Tate: "Me beating the crap out of her is the best thing that has happened to her, because she's made a whole career and living out of it."

On Floyd Mayweather, Jr.: "He would definitely beat me in a boxing match. I unfortunately don't get into matches. I fight for a living."

Alexis Davis: "I'm going to beat Alexis Davis then take a nap."

On Bethe Correia: "I want to beat her in the most devastatingly embarrassing way possible."

On Cris "Cyborg" Justino: "She can fight at 145 pumped full of steroids and she can make weight just like everybody else without them."

But when it came time to promote her fight against Zingano at UFC 184, Rousey was reserved on her comments about her opponent. She was very sensitive to not only Zingano's skillset, but also to her personal circumstances.

"She's the most well-rounded fighter that I've come across," she said. "She has the best mentality of any opponent I've come across yet."

But a lot of fans and observers of the sport took Ronda's kindness toward Cat as a sign that perhaps Cat was, in fact, going to be the one to finally dethrone the champion. That Ronda was being humble because deep down she knew that Cat had her number.

Ronda submitted Zingano with an armbar in just 14 seconds.

It was this fight more than any that created a super-human aura around Rousey. Here was Cat Zingano with a full camp, injury free, and presumably in a better mental state than she was against Nunes, whom she beat to become the No. 1 contender, and Rousey broke more of a sweat walking out to the Octagon than she did inside of it.

Inexplicably, Zingano rushed Rousey and took her down. On the way to the canvas, Rousey reversed

Ronda Rousey, right, consoles Cat Zingano after Zingano tapped out 14 seconds into a UFC 184 title bout.

positions and improvised some kind of backward armbar, and Zingano quickly tapped.

Ronda knelt next to Zingano and hugged her after the tap, and told her she would be happy to do it again. Zingano said as much in her post-fight interview with UFC commentator Joe Rogan.

"I wanna do it again," she said. "I just... [expletive]."

The issue of suicide came up again in her next fight, when Brazilian muay thai specialist Bethe Correia said that Ronda was a phony who blamed everyone else for her own shortfalls, and she cited many things she could have only known about from reading Rousey's autobiography. She went on to say that when she beats Rousey she hopes she "doesn't kill herself."

After so much publicity surrounding the suicide of Ronda's father, it was obvious to everyone, especially Ronda, what Correia was referring to. Ronda vowed to send a message to all future opponents that her family is off limits in any fight hype, saying, "I need to make sure nobody ever tries that again."

Correia, for her part, said she wasn't aware of Ronald Rousey's suicide, and chalked up the poorly worded hype talk to a loss in translation (she speaks Portuguese).

Ronda, and pretty much everyone else, didn't buy that argument. Ronda knocked Bethe unconscious in 34 seconds of the first round, after a fierce exchange.

Just as Ronda predicted she would do, the beatdown was both devastating, and now, embarrassing.

Ronda was originally announced to fight Miesha Tate for a third time in her next title defense after Correia, but Rousey made an appearance on ABC's *Good Morning America* and made a surprise announcement.

"January 2, I will be fighting Holly Holm, who is actually the most

Ronda Rousey chats with UFC President Dana White during her workout at Glendale Fighting Club.

decorated striker we have in all of mixed martial arts," she said. "She is definitely my biggest challenge to date so I'm super excited about it."

The news came as a shock to the MMA world, especially Tate, who didn't find out about the change of plan until after Rousey's morning television announcement. It was also the first time any UFC fight would be announced on such a national platform. And with Robin Roberts, Amy Robach, Ginger Zee, and Lara Spencer all sharing hosting and anchoring duties—with George Stephanopoulos usually the only male on the set—it wasn't a surprise to see Ronda share the stage with such strong and accomplished women.

The Holm fight was originally scheduled for January 2, 2016,

Ronda Rousey training her striking with trainer Edmond Tarverdyan at Glendale Fighting Club.

at the MGM Grand in Las Vegas, Nevada. However, after an injury to welterweight-champion Robbie Lawler's thumb created some opportunities to move things around, UFC brass decided to move up Rousey's championship fight to November 15, 2015, at Melbourne, Australia's Etihad Stadium.

"She will break the all-time attendance record for the sport of mixed martial arts," White told ESPN. "Ronda Rousey was huge for us down in Brazil. She was well received there, it was just a phenomenal event. It did very well on pay-per-view here in the United States. She's obviously a huge superstar for us and Australia is an important market for us so we're going to bring her out there. [It will be] our first big stadium show. We know that she'll break the record."

If White is correct, then the card, which is already a blockbuster, would have to top UFC 129's attendance of 55,724 at Toronto's Rogers Centre, when former welterweight-kingpin and Canadian-superstar Georges St-Pierre successfully defended his title against Jake Shields in 2011.

Holly Holm is an American boxer who had a professional record of 33–2–3 (9 KOs) when she retired in 2013 and entered mixed martial arts full-time. She won both of her UFC fights by unanimous decision, and both were lackluster affairs. However, that doesn't mean she isn't worthy of a title fight. She is undefeated in MMA, and as a renowned striker who has faced the top women in the world of boxing, she'll be a formidable opponent for Rousey.

In a sport where virtually anything can happen in a fight, Holm is poised for one of the biggest upsets in the sport. What separates Holm from a lot of the other talent in the women's bantamweight division is her big-game experience. To paraphrase Chael Sonnen's foreword to this book, she has international experience and has fought under the lights. She is and has been a competitor at the highest level (boxing).

In an MMA fight, the slightest mistake could end the bout. Mixed martial arts fighters compete with four-ounce gloves, and a well-timed punch to the chin or to the back of an ear could change the trajectory of the fight. In boxing, fighters are given standing eight counts and sent back in to fight after a knockdown. In MMA, fighters can follow their opponents down to the ground and try to finish the fight with a flurry of punches, elbows, or submissions.

Holm, for her part, has no delusions about what she's getting into.

"She's got a well-rounded game," she said of Rousey. "I'm not going in there thinking, 'Oh I only have to worry about, you know, grappling.' I do know she has knockout power, so I don't feel like you guys are going to see what you've seen before with her. I fear everything about her. Standup, ground, clinch, all that. And I feel like that's the way you need to be with any fighter."

It's a healthy outlook on a fight with a competitor such as Rousey, and perhaps the maturest outlook on what many believe is an insurmountable task for any opponent. Most others talk a lot of platitudes when describing their mindset or game plan against the Baddest Woman on the Planet.

Holm isn't trying to psych herself up for the fight. She believes she can win, and she has the footwork and the standup skills to keep Rousey at bay in a way that perhaps we've never seen before. But now I sound like every other pundit speculating on some kind of "untested" position "Rowdy" might find herself in. Like the rest, she will likely pass the Holly Holm test in spectacularly quick and devastatingly violent fashion. ■

Ronda poses with 3-year-old Aden Gutierrez after a public workout at the UFC gym in preparation for her bout with Liz Carmouche.

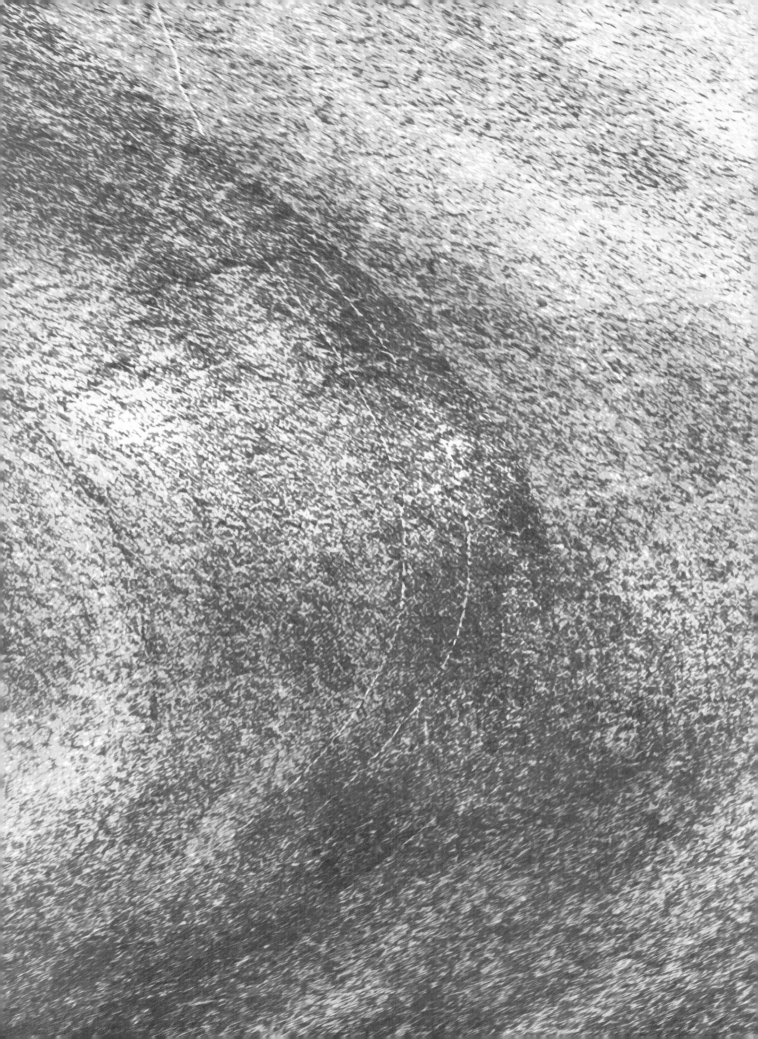

chapter five

Ronda Goes to Hollywood

> "I'm selfish, impatient, and a little insecure. I make mistakes, I am out of control, and at times hard to handle. But if you can't handle me at my worst, then you sure as hell don't deserve me at my best."
>
> —Marilyn Monroe

Getting into the UFC is one of the hardest things any professional mixed martial artist—man or woman—can do. But for a woman to be not only the first ever to be signed to the UFC, but to end up as the organization's biggest worldwide draw, is a Rousey-esque feat.

So it's only fitting that the next industry in Ronda's sights is Hollywood.

Action movies were once dominated by hokey actors with characters who were super-human. If you go back and watch Chuck Norris, Jean Claude Van Damme, Steven Seagal, and even Bruce Lee, there are so many unrealistic

scenes of martial arts stunts that the films, no matter how beloved they were in their day, simply do not hold up.

Why would anyone pay $15 for a movie ticket to watch fake fight choreography when one can tune into any number of MMA events or reality shows and watch the real thing for free?

So it's no wonder that Hollywood screenwriters and directors are increasingly looking to professional MMA fighters to fill roles that were once reserved for pretty actors and their stunt doubles.

Ronda rocks the red carpet at the 2015 ESPY Awards.

Steven Soderbergh cast Strikeforce women's bantamweight champion Gina Carano to star in *Haywire*, an action film about a secret agent whose agency turns against her. While Randy Couture

Ronda Rousey is all smiles as she arrives at the premiere of *Furious 7* on April 1, 2015 in Los Angeles.

and Cung Le were starring in films long before Carano tried her hand at acting, their movies were the standard action movie fare. With Soderbergh at the helm, and a cast including Michael Fassbender and Ewan McGregor, there was something lofty in Carano's casting. The MMA community had a sense of pride that one of ours could be taken seriously enough as an actor to participate with such company.

There were also some disasters along the way. Quinton "Rampage" Jackson starred as B.A. Baracus in the big screen version of *The A-Team*—the role made famous by Mr. T in the campy 1980s TV show. The film was universally panned, and Jackson, while making a nice paycheck, will likely be relegated to roles where he will play the heavy, with not much acting required.

Ronda Jean Rousey's first foray into the world of film was big.

After several meetings with Sylvester Stallone, she was cast

Jason Statham, Harrison Ford, Mel Gibson, Sylvester Stallone, Wesley Snipes, and Ronda Rousey ride a tank during a photo call for *The Expendables 3*. Rousey has turned her celebrity and charisma into a budding career as an action film star.

in *The Expendables 3* as one of the team of mercenaries recruited by Kelsey Grammer and Stallone to lend a bit of youth to the aging action stars that included Stallone, Arnold Schwarzenegger, Jason Statham, Wesley Snipes, Harrison Ford, Dolph Lundgren, Randy Couture, and Mel Gibson.

Rousey played Luna, and IMDB describes her character a such:

At the ESPY Awards UFC fighter Ronda Rousey accepts the Best Female Athlete award.

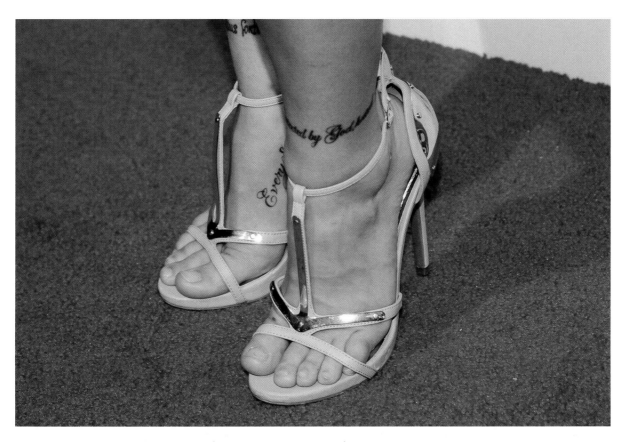

Ronda shows off her pedicure but describes her feet as gnarly after years of Judo and several broken toes.

Discovered by Barney Ross while working as a fierce nightclub bouncer, Luna was immediately recruited into the Expendables. She is an expert at close quarters physical combat and an effective decoy during covert operations. Fun Fact: Luna might be the only female member of The Expendables but she could get every one of them to tap out (well, except maybe Toll Road).

Toll Road is played by UFC Hall of Famer Randy Couture, and I'm not so sure she couldn't tap Couture with her armbar.

Ronda and Ludacris arrive at the premiere of *Furious 7* at the TCL Chinese Theatre IMAX in April 2015, in Los Angeles.

Ronda poses with Jeremy Piven–also known as Ari Gold–at the *Entourage* premiere.

Incidentally, one of the advantages of ground submission moves, like armbars and triangle chokes, is with the proper technique, size or strength is not really an advantage.

Ronda is represented by Brad Slater of the William Morris Endeavor agency, the same agent who helped guide Dwayne "The Rock" Johnson's transition from WWE to Hollywood. WME is also run by Ari Emanuel, the man *Entourage*'s "Ari Gold" character, played by Jeremy Piven, is modeled on (which may or may not have had something to do with Rousey's casting in *Entourage*).

It is no coincidence that Dana White and the UFC itself is represented by WME (Lance Klein has long repped the promotion in media rights deals).

While *The Expendables 3*'s reviews ranged from polite to downright bad, Rousey herself received praise among the entertainment press, with even Rocky Balboa himself touting his ingenue:

"Ronda is absolutely a phenomenon. She's beautiful. She's tough. And she's original. Outspoken. Very fresh. Not guarded. We're lucky to have her," said Stallone.

Next up for Rousey were roles in *Furious 7* and *Entourage.*

In *Furious 7*, Rousey plays Kara. It's an uneventful role that was mostly overshadowed by the tragic death of franchise star Paul Walker. The film did gangbusters at the box office, raking in over $1 billion worldwide. Despite having a lesser role than the one she had in *The Expendables 3*, being associated with such a boffo movie is always a good thing to have on one's résumé.

Kara has a fight scene with Michelle Rodriguez, one of the franchise stars. In the film, director James Wan incorporates moves that Rousey is known for in her fights, like armbars,

Ronda Rousey shines at the Warner Bros. premiere of *Entourage* at Regency Village Theatre on June 1, 2015. Rousey appeared as herself in the film.

superman punches, and muay thai knees (although if I'm not mistaken, Rousey hasn't thrown any superman punches in any of her UFC fights yet). But what's different about this fight is Rousey does it in a gorgeous gold gown, while Rodriguez is beautiful in a red dress and heels.

If beating up Liz Carmouche to defend her UFC belt for the first time was Ronda's early defining moment of her MMA career, then *Entourage* will go down as the beginning of her acting career. In just her third big screen role, Rousey was cast as herself, and it was her best role yet. (It's been reported Rousey will play herself in a screen adaptation of her autobiography, and *Entourage* serves as a fine forecast for her prospects in such an endeavor.)

In *Entourage*, Rousey meets Turtle (Jerry Ferrara), who asks Rousey out on a date. Rousey, tired of the attention she receives out in public, invites him over for dinner at her apartment. But on the day of the date, Drama (Kevin Dillon) convinces Turtle that Rousey would never be interested in him. So, Turtle decides to pitch Ronda on a business proposition (out of insecurity), and Rousey throws him out of her place.

Turtle, furious with Drama, tries in vain to get a second date, and shows up at Rousey's gym, where

MMA champion Ronda Rousey after making an appearance on *Jimmy Kimmel Live*.

she is training with her real-life team (together dubbed The Four Horsewomen)—Jessamyn Duke (who was on Ronda's TUF team), Marina Shafir (Ronda's real-life roommate and judo training partner), and Shayna Baszler (a pioneer of women's MMA).

Rousey tells Turtle he can have a second date if he can last more than 30 seconds in the Octagon with her. Turtle agrees, but is quickly put into an armbar, and since he refuses to tap out, she snaps his arm.

Rousey talks to Robin Roberts on ABC's *Good Morning America* in New York in March 2015.

The good news for Turtle, however, is that he lasts more than 30 seconds and gets his second date (albeit with his arm in a sling).

The scene gets a great laugh, but more important, even though most athletes who play themselves end up looking kind of foolish, Rousey remains a badass with some comedy chops to boot.

While most critics unanimously hated the film, most agreed that Rousey came off better than average, no small feat for an amateur actress in only her third role, playing against a cast that has worked together for some eight seasons.

Suffice it to say Ronda is nowhere near done with Hollywood, and is reportedly going to take time off after her Holly Holm fight on November 15, 2015, to film a starring role in yet another big budget film.

In 2014, Rousey became the first UFC fighter to win an ESPY (Female Athlete of the Year). Previously, fighters like Georges St-Pierre and Frankie Edgar were nominated for the honor, but so far Rousey is the only one to take home not one, but two awards.

In 2015, Rousey took yet another step when she won the ESPY for Fighter of Year.

On the red carpet, Rousey took a verbal jab at Floyd Mayweather, Jr., outright wondering how he feels actually "getting beat by a woman for once," a not-so-subtle jab at his domestic abuse charges. "Try acting like you don't know who I am now," she said, looking directly into camera.

The feud between the two most dominant fighters in their respective sports started in 2014, when Rousey was nominated for the Fighter of Year ESPY. When asked how he felt going up a against a woman for the honor, he feigned ignorance. "Ron Rousey? I don't know who he is," Mayweather said.

Sylvester Stallone, Ronda Rousey, and Arnold Schwarzenegger on the red carpet for the Macau, China premiere of their movie *The Expendables 3* on August 22, 2014.

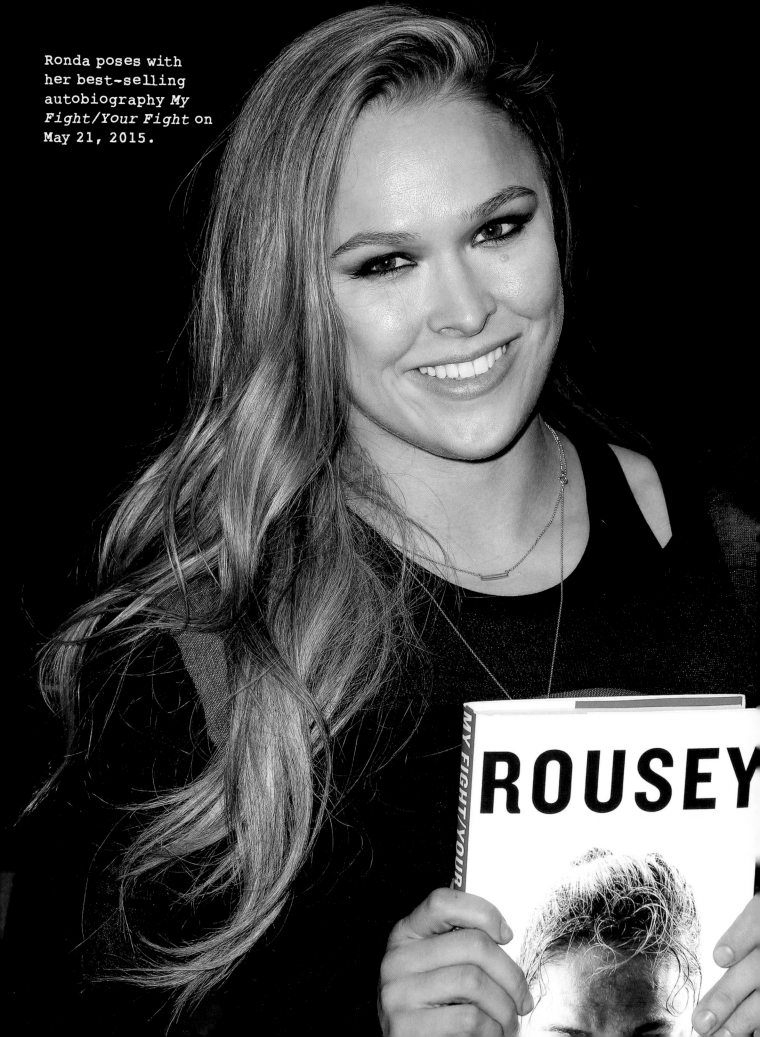

Ronda poses with her best-selling autobiography *My Fight/Your Fight* on May 21, 2015.

Rousey waited a whole year to respond.

"I know for damn sure that he knew who I was, because he was running against me for Best Fighter that year and he has signed MMA fighters," Rousey said. "So his feigned ignorance was meant to be a snarky remark to me."

After Rousey beat Correia in just 34 seconds by knockout in the very first round, sports media started to openly wonder who would win a fight between Mayweather and Rousey (let's face it, that will never happen and should never happen).

Even super bantamweight boxing champion Maureen Shea said she would have Ronda in a fight against Mayweather. "She would rip his arm off," said Shea.

But as for Ronda coming into boxing and immediately becoming successful, Shea was a bit more doubtful. "If you're asking about Ronda's boxing abilities, I think given the type of athlete she is, if she gives a significant amount of time training as a boxer, I think she'd be an amazing boxer," Shea said. "But not right now. She is going to have to train for a period of time. You don't just walk into my sport and say that 'I'm going to do what you're going to do,' but her athleticism, her desire to win, I respect every ounce of it. And you know, if she gives it the time, and just trains straight-up boxing, I think she would do really well."

Mayweather, whose nickname is "Money," reverted to what he always reverts to when he's faced with any real challenge to his manhood: his money. Not surprisingly, he was ignorant, as usual.

"I've yet to see any MMA fighter, or other boxer, make over $300 million in 36 minutes," Mayweather said on ESPN's *SportsCenter.* "When she can do that, then call me."

Ronda was quick to respond, and like most of her fights, she ended it quickly for the win.

"I actually did the math and given the numbers of my last fight, I'm actually the highest paid UFC fighter and I'm a woman." She adds, "I actually make two-to-three times more than he does per second. When he learns to read and write, he can text me."

When Mayweather started in on UFC's pay scale for its fighters, the promotion used its Twitter account (with its 2.4 million followers) to respond with a 16 second video showing some of Ronda's fierce judo throws and ending with her toss and then nine unanswered punches to Alexis Davis' face, as UFC play-by-play announcer Mike Goldberg screams "It is all over. Just. Like. That!"

The hashtag—#SheDontNeed12Rounds —was another dig at Mayweather.

Since the Correia fight, mainstream media can't get enough of Rousey. *CBS This Morning*, *Good Morning America*, *Today*, ESPN, FOX Sports, TMZ, Gawker, Vice, the *New York Times*, the *Los Angeles Times*, Jimmy Kimmel, Jimmy Fallon—you name it, they are either interviewing her, or finding any reason to mention her.

Her autobiography became a best seller in its first week of release. Thousands of girls are dressing like her for Halloween.

As of this writing, Rousey is just 28 years old, in a sport that has only been around for a little more than 20 years, in a women's division barely three years old, and she is one of the world's biggest stars. ■

Ronda poses, relaxed, three days prior to her UFC debut fight against Liz Carmouche on February 23, 2013.

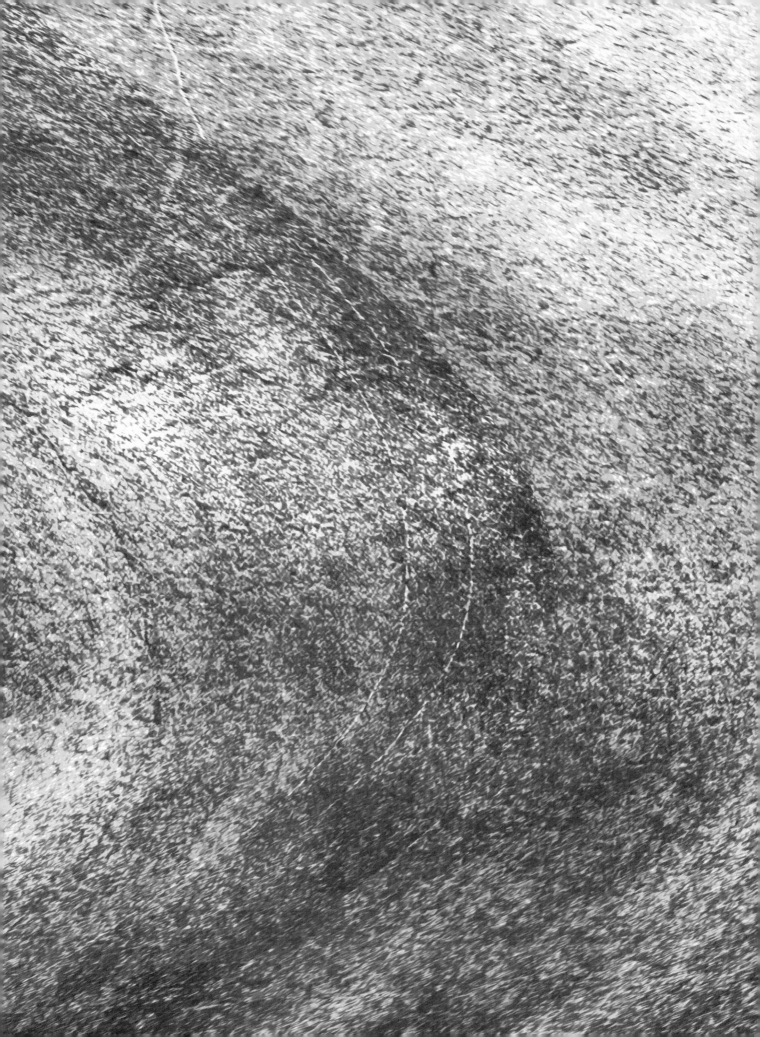

chapter six

Ronda in Her Own Words

"Don't be a do-nothing bitch!"
—Ronda Rousey

Ronda is what I like to call a sound-bite machine.

She is never at a loss for words, and she comes off as if she's rehearsed every potential question and every possible answer.

In fact, when she was preparing her first really big media conference call with Miesha Tate, she did just that. In her autobiography she writes that she practiced responses to hypothetical questions posed to her by her friends and her mother.

Before the Bethe Correia fight, Rousey was asked by a FOX Sports crew if she had a response to men who criticize her physique as being too masculine. Ronda had a few choice words for the men and women who put too much emphasis on appearances—also known as "body shamers."

"Just because my body was developed for a purpose other than [expletive] millionaires doesn't mean it's masculine. I think it's femininely badass as [expletive], because there's not a single muscle on my body that isn't for a purpose. Because I'm not a do-nothing bitch."

The quote went viral, with t-shirts being sold by Represent Clothing with a picture of Rousey sitting on the edge of her bed in a sports bra and shorts and her hands on her head, abs shining and biceps flexing with the caption "Don't Be A D.N.B." emblazoned on the front.

Ronda has never shied away from admitting that many of her catch phrases are co-opted from her mother. One of her strongest quotes is truly what she lives every day of her life.

Rousey talks about her upcoming championship fight during media day for UFC 184 at Glendale Fighting Club.

"You're not training to be the best in the world. You're training to be the best in the world on your worst day."

I've been around the fight business long enough to know that no fighter, man or woman, ever competes at 100 percent. It's nearly impossible to do so after a six-week training camp in which you're sparring, grappling, lifting, running, dieting, and punishing your body in myriad ways in order to prepare to enter a cage where someone is planning—no, *being paid*—to punish you in new ways.

Trainer Edmond Tarverdyan lo●sens Ronda's shoulder at the UFC open workout in Brazil.

So many fighters who lose like to come out and announce some nagging injury that they never mentioned before the fight, in order to save face for the loss. I've seen fighters who know better than to do it, do it. It's like they can't help themselves.

When Manny Pacquiao lost to Floyd Mayweather in a one-sided beatdown, he immediately announced that he was fighting with a shoulder injury that will require surgery, sparking an investigation by the Nevada State Athletic Commission and at least one class action lawsuit on behalf of gamblers who put money on Manny to win.

Ronda is undefeated in fights, but she once took a fight with stitches in her foot, a result of a dog bite. She was able to hide the stitches while weighing in, and then won her fight in a matter of seconds so that she wouldn't do any more damage to her foot. In judo, she has competed—and won, with a broken foot, the flu, broken fingers, and food poisoning.

That's a result of preparing to be the best in the world on your worst day.

"The problem isn't me thinking I can achieve any goal I set for myself, the problem is you projecting your own self-doubt onto me."

Whether it was judo, mixed martial arts, or now acting, Rousey has defied the odds, and she's done it on her own terms. Everyone who has ever accomplished anything, whether it's straight A's in school, a volleyball team trophy, a prom date, a boyfriend or girlfriend, a military award, a job—you name it, there are always going to be people rooting against you. Even some of your family and your closest friends. Jealousy is an unfortunate part of human nature. Misery does love company.

But it takes a champion's attitude to plow through that negative energy. Rousey has endured negative energy from her judo peers, old trainers, her managers at the bar and at the gym where she worked the overnight shift, her boyfriends who put her down for her muscular physique, and the girlfriends who were jealous.

Most recently a former model took to social media to blast Rousey for dating her ex. Ronda has to stay above the fray. She has to put her head down and keep moving forward. She does this over and over again even though it gets old. It gets hard. She cries. She glares.

She clenches her teeth. And through it all, she wins. She has seen her bank account go from negative dollars to millions of dollars, an apartment that spewed sewage onto her carpet and clothing to a luxury beachfront property, and her filthy dirty car with one missing side-rear mirror from an accident, to a German sports car. Through it all, she wins.

"A loss leads to a victory. Being fired leads to a dream job. A death leads to a birth. I find comfort in believing that good things can come out of tragedy."

Ronda Rousey practicing her left hook with trainer Edmond Tarverdyan. That left hook is what knocked out Bethe Correia at UFC 190 in Rio de Janeiro.

When Ronda didn't win a gold medal at the 2008 Olympics (she took bronze), she was heartbroken, but through that heartbreak grew an even deeper desire to win. An Olympic gold medalist Ronda Rousey may not have ever been UFC champion Ronda Rousey.

Ronda was a swimmer in her youth, but the solitude of the sport made her think of her father, made her wonder why things had to be the way they were, and it made her sad.

She quit swimming and found judo. Through all of life's downs, Ronda, whether she knew it or not, would persevere and go further than even she ever imagined. When she got into a car accident on a Los Angeles freeway, she sat on the side of the road with a broken nose and blood in her hair and streaming down her chin. She called her mother and said, "I hate this part of the book." Even at her lowest, she foreshadowed greatness worthy of a biography. It just so happens it would be a best-selling book less than 10 years later.

Let that sink in for a minute.

"I'm scared of failure all the time but not scared enough to stop trying."

An artist should never judge himself or herself. If Leonardo da Vinci waited to be perfect, nobody would have ever laid eyes on the *Mona Lisa*. If Frank Sinatra never sang a note until he was perfect, he would have been an anonymous firefighter, maybe, in Hoboken, New Jersey. If William Shakespeare waited until he wrote the perfect play, *Romeo and Juliet* wouldn't have inspired dozens of star-struck romance stories, and if Bruce Springsteen never sang one of his lyrics because he feared failure, he would still be in New Jersey, too, probably complaining that cars don't have carburetors anymore.

So many athletes, actors, musicians, painters, writers, designers, engineers, and scientists fear failure, and that fear of failure is what prevents them from ever succeeding. Don't let the fear of failure cripple you. Don't let the derision of lesser people drive you into the dark.

Rousey walks to a meeting with New York Governor Andrew Cuomo and state leaders where she urges them to join the 49 other states in legalizing mixed martial arts.

Great actors will tell you that a great scene is not about the payoff, but about the little moments along the journey. Live in the moment, and greatness will happen, sometimes by accident and sometimes by design.

"Most girls didn't have a world champ walking around the house like I did, and that showed me anything was possible. If I can provide that to anyone else, that would be awesome."

Like most teenagers, Rousey rebelled against her mother on many occasions. She ran away from home to go live in upstate New York and train judo. From there she spent time in Montreal, and even lived in Chicago with a boyfriend who put her down in order to make himself feel better. But through it all Dr. AnnMaria De Mars always kept the door open for Ronda.

It's easy now for Ronda to look back and give her mother credit, but would she if things hadn't turned out so well? If she ever did just give up on herself, would she have blamed her mother for being a world champion? For putting too much pressure on her to live up to her? Would she have risen above her shadow? We all know the answer, but the truth is, De Mars let Ronda fall flat on her face time and time again, and perhaps the greatest gift she gave her was to let her pick herself up time and time again.

Ronda expected that tough love, and when she lost early in the 2004 Olympics, she feared facing her mother the most. But it was De Mars who simply hugged Ronda and told her that she hadn't failed. "You just had a bad day," she said. It is this kind of balance that has stuck with Rousey all of these years.

Tough love with a tiny bit of compassion has served Ronda well.

Ronda Rousey relaxes after a tough workout.

Ronda Rousey stretches during her July 15, 2015 workout at Glendale Fighting Club.

"I'm living such a lucky and blessed life, and I'm trying my best to deserve it, so thank you. I'll be back here, just you watch."

Rousey said those words as she stood at the podium in front of an audience of some of the greatest athletes in the world at the 2015 ESPY Awards. Even in a moment of triumph, Ronda was looking forward to earning the honor once again, vowing to be back. Most athletes vow to be back only after a loss. "I'll come back strong," is a common mantra in the loser's post-fight interview. But to say "I'll be back here" after a win?

That's some kind of tunnel vision.

"People say to me all the time, 'You have no fear.' I tell them, 'No, that's not true. I'm scared all the time.' You have to have fear in order to have courage. I'm a courageous person because I'm a scared person."

Every time Ronda wins a fight, mostly in under a minute, she takes her mouthpiece out of her mouth and smiles. If she could do a "happy dance" she probably would, but it's probably not a good look for her in front of millions of people. A happy dance might backfire on the Baddest Woman on the Planet. But the point is, that smile is always so telling, no matter how dominant she is in her victory.

The smile is almost a look of surprise. Ronda is scared to lose. That's why she tries so hard. That's why she trains so hard. Ronda hates losing more than she likes winning, if that makes any sense at all. But the thing is, Ronda knows what it is like to lose. She may be undefeated in her amateur and professional mixed martial arts career, but as ironic as this may seem, even though it is the sport of MMA that makes her millions of dollars and world famous, Ronda still respects judo more than she does MMA. After all, in judo she has lost. In a way, Ronda destroys her opponents just to show the world how difficult competing in judo is.

It's like she's saying, "I lost in judo. Do you know how easy this is now?"

"When I was in school, martial arts made you a dork, and I became self-conscious that I was too masculine. I was a 16-year-old girl with ringworm and cauliflower ears. People made fun of my arms and called me 'Miss Man.' It wasn't until I got older that I realized: These people are idiots. I'm fabulous."

Body shamers. They are yet another negative outshoot of the Internet age. In the general digital age they are called trolls. In the world of MMA, they're called keyboard warriors. There are any number of keyboard warriors out there. Some work as bloggers on sites which are now owned by big media companies but left unchecked by their new corporate bosses, and the boys who used to blog about MMA in their underwear are suddenly "journalists."

In July 2014, Ronda Rousey poses during a weigh-in for UFC 175 at the Mandalay Bay in Las Vegas.

These clowns get off on spewing hate and vitriol on anyone more successful than they are, and unfortunately, famous women athletes are no different.

Rousey grew up in the age of haters. Neil Strauss wrote an entire book on how to pick up women, and the number one tactic is something called "The Neg," in which the game is to put down a woman so that she tries real hard to get him to like her.

Even Serena Williams has been the subject of body shaming, sometimes by her rivals' coaches. Top 10 tennis star Agnieszka Radwanska's coach Tomasz Wiktorowski, said about his charge, "It's our decision to keep her as the smallest player in the top 10. Because, first of all she's a woman, and she wants to be a woman," and the *New York Times* wrote: "Williams, who will be vying for the Wimbledon title against Garbiñe Muguruza on Saturday, has large biceps and a mold-breaking muscular frame, which packs the power and athleticism that have dominated women's tennis for years. Her rivals could try to emulate her physique, but most of them choose not to."

Really?

Serena Williams is the greatest tennis player of all time. It's no coincidence that Ronda is the greatest MMA fighter of all time, and they're both women. They're beautiful and powerful, and they choose not to be "do-nothing bitches." It's a shame to think that other women athletes would trade overwhelming success in order to fit someone else's idea of how they should look.

"You know what? I would beat the crap out of Kim Kardashian actually. Any girl who is famous and idolized because she made a sex video with some guy and that's all that you're known for, 'Oh, I got my fame for [expletive],' I think it's pretty stupid. Sorry, but it's true."

Women like Kim Kardashian and Paris Hilton are in a category all their own, and while it's not their fault that they became famous by behaving badly, Rousey is right to condemn their kind of fame. That's not to say both Hilton and Kardashian weren't right to run all the way to the bank with their so-called stardom. They've both made fortunes

123

after landing on the gossip pages for outrageous antics. Rousey chooses to earn her fortune by winning fights with her body, and not being used for it.

When Kardashian heard what Rousey thought of her, she told a reporter "I think she's really beautiful, and I don't want to say anything bad about her." Rousey responded, "What could she say? I think the best move for her is to not piss me off any more."

"If you have good legs under you, then you can punch. Anybody can stand and throw their hands and look like an idiot. If you actually want to learn how to punch, you have to work on being balanced on your legs and feeling your legs under you. Feel the ground. I wasn't allowed to throw big hooks and overhand rights until I'd been striking for three years. It's so you don't rely on those things from the very beginning. If your footwork sucks and you can only stand in one place and throw your hands all crazy while the other person is running around, you're never going to be able to hit them. So what's the point? You have to have good legs to catch somebody first before you hit them."

Edmond Tarverdyan is the coach who forbade Rousey to throw those punches until she had three years of striking training under her belt, but that hardly kept her from winning fights.

When you're that good that you can win fights by deliberately not trying to knock your opponent out, that's a scary proposition. Ronda Rousey is the perfect student, and luckily for her, she found the perfect coach who knew how to bring her along, while not holding her back.

Rousey has good legs. She has better hips. Grappling is all about

Ronda Rousey shares a laugh with fans at a book signing for her autobiography *My Fight/Your Fight.*

hips. Keeping them lower than your opponent's so you're not easily rolled over or thrown. There's no question that years of elite judo has prepared Rousey for her MMA career better than any other course of training could have.

In MMA we have a saying. "The sport passed him by." That means that younger people trained different and became more "rounded" as a mixed martial artist. They say the sport passed Matt Hughes by, who won mostly with his dominant wrestling.

When Georges St-Pierre came along, he was more well-rounded as a fighter, with better striking and jiu-jitsu. He dethroned Hughes. Frankie Edgar came along and beat up B.J. Penn to take his lightweight title. Frankie was more of a complete fighter than B.J., but Penn took out all of his contemporaries. Rashad Evans knocked out Chuck Liddell with a more dynamic striking game. Lyoto Machida knocked out Randy Couture with some ninja moves. Mixed martial arts is a sport that is constantly evolving.

It's safe to say, however, that the sport will not ever pass Ronda Rousey by. No, she will be collecting Oscars while the next great female fighter is wiping the mat with opponent after opponent. And by the time the next-next big thing comes along, Rousey will likely be collecting a Nobel Prize, or writing another best-selling book, or perhaps, running for office.

Whatever Ronda Rousey decides is worth fighting for, she will most certainly win. ◼

Rousey at the Cannes Film Festival in France in May 2014.

Glen Powell, Ronda Rousey, and Kelsey Grammer during a photo call for *The Expendables 3* at the 67th international film festival in Cannes, France on May 18, 2014.

Acknowledgments

Thanks goes out to Frank and Elizabeth Straka; David Shaw; Gill Torren; David Snow; Thomas Gerbasi; Chael Sonnen; Renzo Gracie; Harris Masood; Triumph Books' Jesse Jordan, Adam Motin, Michelle Green, Mitch Rogatz, Josh Williams, and Noah Amstadter; Alex Sassaris of Pinks bar in the East Village and Giuseppe Delli Carpini of Little Italy restaurant Margherita—which both served as my offices while writing this book; and to everyone at Renzo Gracie Academy in New York City for keeping me in check.

And thank you Ronda Rousey. Your story inspires me every day.